INVISIBLE FREEDOM

Find Strength in Self-Love
to Pursue Healthy Relationships

Decole Pearson
"CocoaDecole"

Copyright @2021 Decole "CocoaDecole" Pearson

All rights reserved. No part of this publication may be reproduced, distributed, or transmitted in any form or by any means, including photocopying, recording, or other electronic or mechanical methods, without the prior written permission of the publisher, except in the case of brief quotations, embodied in reviews and certain other non-commercial uses permitted by copyright law.

ISBN: 978-1-7363337-09

DEDICATION

This book is dedicated to my husband, my children, my mother (ride or die), my dad, my pops, my sisters, my brothers, and my nephews, and my nieces. A special dedication to my amazing God-fearing grandmothers, Johnnie Woolridge and Notie B. Hall, and my late grandfather Napoleon Hall. Two of my uncles, Johnny E. and Tim G. I would not be who I am without all of you. I hope to continue to break generational curses, encourage, uplift, and inspire. God, I am nothing without you.

FOREWORD

When I began to read the introduction of *Invisible Freedom*, written by Decole, or Cocoa as many affectionately call her, I immediately smiled! My smile was inspired by her words. I heard her, the tone of Cocoa's voice echoing in my head. As the words in the intro jumped off the page, it clearly defined and brought to my remembrance the young Sistahgirl I met in 1997. The introduction and reflections reminded me of the fast, lifelong connection we made and what I know to be her journey.

Cocoa walked into her future place of employment unbeknownst to her for Community Service. At the time, I was the Community Service Coordinator at our beloved East Oakland Youth Development Center and would verify the Community Service hours Decole completed. Decole continued volunteering afterwards and was eventually offered a receptionist position. We both have a spirit of helping others. Cocoa and I walked into a Sistaship newly formed between us. Today we are Sistahs from other Mothers!

As you read through the chapters of this book, you too will connect with Cocoa and for various right reasons. Cocoa is a Beautiful Black Woman who is real, loves her people real hard, is definitely family oriented and a loyal Sistahfriend. Cocoa is a mentee and mentor, readily and knowingly accepting those assigned to her.

Cocoa has lived what some may call the non-traditional childhood and championed the teenage years of growing up in Oakland, CA. As a young Black teenager and woman growing up, one can find themselves exposed to the fast, hustle life which Oakland is known for—Bay Area!! Cocoa had the ability to successfully navigate through her teen and young adult years with multiple distractions that hit close to home. In a city where the teen pregnancy rate for young Black girls and women was soaring, the high school dropout rate an embarrassment and young Black boys and men standing at the crossroads of life or death, Cocoa navigated well. She has experienced relationships on the road to being gifted with her true love and marriage to a wonderful Man and Father of her children for more than 20 years. A wonderful mother to two and a bonus mother for two additional children. Cocoa is a dedicated Mother committed to the healthy development and growth of her beautiful children. Cocoa is a humble caregiver to those in her family, a devoted worthy daughter, granddaughter and sibling.

As Cocoa moved around in employment, she discovered her niche of helping others. I have had the opportunity to quietly witness Cocoa grow through multiple stages that we all may encounter in life.

I encourage you to read this book and trust the process. Completing the exercises in this book may take a little deep breathing at times to push through but it will be worth it. Those you engage in relationships with will also benefit from the changes they see in you for the better. Consider yourself in good company for choosing *Invisible Freedom*.

Kim "KayCeeitsme" Coleman, Poet & Writer

TABLE OF CONTENTS

Cocoadecole's Prayer	1
Introduction	3
Chapter 1: *Who Are You?*	11
Chapter 2: *What's Your Relationship with God?*	17
Chapter 3: *Forgiveness and Healing*	23
Chapter 4: *Me, Myself, and I*	31
Chapter 5: *Preparation*	37
Chapter 6: *The Power of No*	43
Chapter 7: *Patience Is a Virtue*	51
Chapter 8: *Wellness Check*	57
Chapter 9: *Effective Communication*	63
Chapter 10: *What's Their Intentions?*	71
Chapter 11: *Friends before Lovers*	79
Chapter 12: *Real Love*	85

Chapter 13: *Love Is in the Air*   91

Chapter 14: *Soar*   97

CocoaDecole's Prayer

Dear God,

I pray that whoever reads this book and completes the exercises, that you bless them, that you show them and teach them how to love themselves. That you help them believe in themselves and learn how to heal and forgive themselves and others.

I ask that you bind up the spirit of fear, self-doubt, anxiety, and depression, and replace it with faith, boldness, love, and understanding. I pray that you do not let them back down and be afraid of no one, fear no one but God. I pray that you let their pain serve a greater purpose and that they can uplift someone else in their journey.

God, I pray that you help them to not lean unto their own understanding, but to acknowledge you so that you can direct their path. I pray that you allow them to prosper. I pray that they live in good health, and that you remove anything from their life that doesn't serve their purpose. I pray that you give them peace of mind and the will to not give up.

In the name of Jesus.

Amen

INTRODUCTION

*"And know my daughter do not fear...
you are a worthy woman."*

Ruth 3:11

When I met my husband in late 1994, I had no idea that our journey together would inspire me to write a book about relationships. In the beginning, my husband and I didn't know anything about how to promote and create a healthy environment. We both just went with the flow of things. We were young and made plenty of mistakes. Neither of us set boundaries. Hell, we didn't even know what boundaries were. We weren't exposed to many healthy relationships growing up, so an overall lack of healthy communication, insecurities, and dysfunction in our environment set the tone.

In our early years of dating, unresolved aspects from our pasts influenced who we were together. For example, my husband lost his mom at the age of 13. As a result, he was afraid he was going to lose anyone he loved and cared for. There were times I wanted to hang out with my friends and he would complain or start arguments to discourage me from going. Of course, we weren't aware that the trauma he had endured needed attention, or that it affected our relationship. Imagine two young adults loving each other and unaware that they both suffered from some form of trauma. How can you heal something that you haven't identified? Growing up in the streets, both of us were forced to grow up fast, without the skills and tools to guide us through. We did not have positive coping skills.

We tried to find ourselves together. Looking back now, we never truly acknowledged that we needed to do the work separately to heal our individual wounds. Instead, through trial and error, we ended up causing more pain, inflicting our past traumas on each other without even knowing it. We didn't know what it looked like to have healthy conversations, or seek relationship support. Instead, we fell into arguing, fighting, and trust issues. We did not know how to communicate effectively and give each other space to grow without being insecure in the process.

As the years went by, I noticed that I slowly started flaking on my friends, one party/social gathering at a time—to prevent arguments. At times, I would stay home on the weekends to be with my two bonus kids, and later our first born. I have to say, it wasn't solely because of my husband's behavior that I lost my way. *I just didn't know who I was.* It took me years to notice that I was deteriorating. I became a homebody, adapting to the *"routine family life" while he kept his social life on the weekends.* The dreams I had of becoming a fashion designer, and other things that inspired me, were not a priority anymore… my family was. No one told me that I could have a family, a healthy relationship, be a great mom, and still live out my dreams. I didn't know that was an option, nor did I know how to create balance.

It's so easy to lose yourself when you lack self-awareness and proper self-love. You compromise your integrity, morals,

INTRODUCTION

principles, and self-respect. In many relationships, people become chameleons, easily adapting to someone else's environment because of their eagerness to be together. Self-consciously, we try to fill the void of the unspoken trauma, of the pain we've encountered throughout the years. If you are not careful to take the time to love yourself properly, you start to lose pieces of yourself without noticing.

It is not until enough time passes that you become unhappy with the status of your life. The things that once brought you joy, like hobbies, furthering your education, shopping, career advancement, and being around people that made your heart smile, no longer have a place in your life. **Why? Because you catered to someone else's agenda.** In many cases, adjusting your lifestyle is necessary for your happily ever after. However, it is also equally important that you don't make a 360-degree turn to please your partner and lie about who you are. These things will not bring you happiness in your relationship.

It is so important to set the tone for how others treat you and establish boundaries in the beginning of all relationships. When you begin the process of loving yourself you promote peace and growth in your life. Boundaries should be non-negotiable and are essential to protecting your mental health and well-being.

I realize that as women, it is easy to put our partners, kids, family, and careers above our own needs. We all want to be the best we can in our relationships, but if it comes at the expense of deceiving ourselves, what good is that? Doing such can cause extreme wear and tear. If that strain persists, your relationship with yourself will deteriorate.

This was true for me. I poured myself into my family and helping others execute their dreams and giving them hope. While it was fulfilling, I lost and neglected myself in the process. It wasn't until I took a good look at my life that I noticed how a lack of self-motivation prevented me from leveling up. I knew that God stored many gifts and talents within me, and it took far too long to discover that I wasn't living my best life, fulfilling my purpose, or loving myself properly.

Now, here I am in my forties realizing that it was **ME** all along. I was waiting for someone else to validate my happiness. I was expecting someone else to do what I needed to do for myself. Through the years, I started to discover myself, and evolve as a woman. I realized the importance of setting boundaries and displaying how I wanted to be treated by my husband, friends, and family. Once I started loving myself the right way, living my dreams and putting myself first, my relationship with my husband evolved and we had more respectful conversations.

So, I have one question to ask you. **Are you standing in the way of you?** I urge you to let today be the day that you vow to know who you are, know what you need, and open yourself to growth and change. As you embark on this journey of self-discovery, it is important to understand that you will never be perfect. You will cry. You will have highs and lows; but it's important that you do not lose faith and give up on yourself. *"Weeping may endure for a night, but Joy cometh in the morning."* (Psalms 30:5, King James Version)

In this book, I'm going to be focused on intimate relationships. I want you to know how you can be in a partnership without losing yourself. However, the skills you will learn are also useful in friendships, relationships at work, or anyone else with whom you might interact with.

As you navigate the chapters of this book, don't hold yourself hostage to your past. Be sure to stand up to the negative voices in

INTRODUCTION

your head that once held you in bondage, preventing you from loving yourself wholeheartedly, and regain control of your destiny. I urge you to love yourself, create boundaries, and speak up for yourself. I urge you to not let fear, anxiety, or anyone's behavior affect the way you see yourself and how you heal.

You may discover that some people will not serve a purpose in your life going forward. This is okay. You will be okay. God said in His word that *"He will never leave you, nor forsake you."*

(I Chronicles 28:20, King James Version)

By the end of this book, I want you to take away having confidence in yourself so that you can truly be *you* in a relationship, and have the tools for navigating the ups and downs of love.

You are enough.

*"Be brave enough to heal yourself
even when it hurts."*

—Bianca Sparacino

CHAPTER 1:
WHO ARE YOU?

"Who are you?" Do you really know who you are? Are you who someone else wants you to be? Have you ever asked yourself these questions?

I hope it provokes some thought about how you currently see yourself, and who you aspire to be, particularly in a relationship. When you know *who you are*, you know who you are not. You are not easily influenced by people's thoughts or agendas that don't have your best interest at heart. You have clarity about someone else's manipulative motives towards you. You create a ground for mutual understandings, and you don't allow others to mold you to their liking.

By knowing who you are, you enter relationships with confidence, self-awareness, and knowing what's best for you. It prevents you from creating a false representation of yourself. It's important that you are being YOU, and not apologizing for being YOU. Knowing who you are is vital to the decisions you make in your life, and who you allow into your life, in order to keep from repeating past mistakes. Knowing who are doesn't mean that you are not open to learning, growing, and evolving within relationships. It means that you've decided not to rely on anyone to validate what you believe about yourself, and not compromise your personal identity for anyone.

INVISIBLE FREEDOM

Knowing who you are is imperative to how you show up in your daily life. You have to understand that energies attract people. So, if you are not clear about who you are, you will meet people based off the hidden energy you're projecting. If you are insecure or have trust issues, there's a possibility you may meet someone who is dominant, insecure, and operating in ego. If you are not careful, they will try to control the narrative of your life out of their own insecurities. You will be moving to the beat of their drum, and that may lead to the road of self-destruction. Don't put your life in the hands of someone who is unclear about who they are, with no direction.

There's a version of you that needs to die and be restored to experience who you were meant to be.

Do you know that any relationship can work? It all depends on what you are willing to put up with. If you are willing to accept anything to make a relationship work—such as cheating, lying, good sex in exchange for bad behavior, being deceived, being taken advantage of, disrespected, financial manipulation—then it's time to go back to the drawing board. You need to understand who you are first.

I want you to think about everything that has brought you to this place of wanting change. In the section below, write down the positive thoughts you tell yourself about who you are. This is important so that in the future, you will learn how to stand bold and firm in who you were born to be.

During this exercise in the chapter *Who Are You?*, the unspoken pain that has been vibrating on the inside of your soul may surface. You're aligning yourself with God's purpose for your life. It is time to unmask your pain and bury the old you. It is time to take control

WHO ARE YOU?

of your life, find strength in your individuality, and create an environment that will forever bring you peace.

Reclaim your life.

INSTRUCTIONS:

Write and fill in positive mindful affirmations about yourself that will address the negative thoughts you may have. Examples of this can include: *I am a child of God, I am loved, I am a Black woman, I am brave, I am forgiving, I am outspoken, I am empathetic, I am compassionate, I am a warrior, I am a protector, I am a wife, I am a mother, I am a friend, I am flawed, etc.*

(Positive Mindful Affirmations)

*Example: I am able to love more, forgive more, be more kind, etc.

Write and repeat to yourself daily

I am _____

I am _____

I am _____

I am _____

I am _____

I am _____

I am _____

I am _____

I am _____

I am _____

I am _____

II Corinthians 12:9

But he said unto me, "My grace is sufficient for you, my power is made perfect in weakness."

CHAPTER 2:
WHAT'S YOUR RELATIONSHIP WITH GOD?

Believing and having a relationship with God will align you for your divine purpose in life. **God is a Redeemer, a Savior, and Rescuer.** God will build your confidence, self-worth, self-esteem, and give you guidance on your journey. But you must have a relationship in order to hear him. Having a true relationship with God will remind you that you are always loved and valued. God works from the inside out so that you can become clear about who you are. In God's word, He said, *"He will never leave you nor forsaken you."* (Deuteronomy 31:6) So, when the mountains in life seem hard to climb, everything you will ever need is within your relationship with God.

You will no longer seek confirmation from others and you will be able to hear God's voice, which ultimately forces you to make decisions that will help you get to the next level in life. One of the amazing things about God is He will make deposits in your life and show you how to love yourself unconditionally. You will no longer be inconsistent and only pray when problems arise; you won't be afraid to talk about God in the presence of others.

Having a solid relationship with God before entering any relationship will allow you to recognize and deny anything or anyone that doesn't look, sound, and or operate like God.

INVISIBLE FREEDOM

As you build your relationship with God, be sure to create an atmosphere to meditate and pray without distractions.

Remember, God is loving, and also forgiving. He loves you for who you are, no matter where you are in your life journey. So, if you've struggled in your relationship with God, strayed away, or time has lapsed in your conversation with Him, He will meet you where you are. God is and has always been by your side… He has just been waiting for you to allow Him in. He will be your personal damage control enforcer, and your greatest teacher. There will be people or things that come into your life to help serve a greater purpose for you to learn, grow, and develop. Even in trial and tribulations, peaks and valleys, God will see you through.

Don't get distracted by people; it's always about God.

As you complete the activity below, it is important that you are honest, vulnerable, and transparent with yourself.

WHAT'S YOUR RELATIONSHIP WITH GOD?

In this exercise, please answer the questions about the chapter *What's Your Relationship with God?*

Question 1: What does a relationship between God and me look like?

Question 2: Why is it important for me to build a relationship with God?

Question 3: How do I grow in my faith in God?

Question 4: Where do I start my relationship with God?

Question 5: Who can I fellowship with?

"Understand that people do the best they can. It may not have been the best for you, but it is the best they knew. Create your best."

—Decole Pearson

CHAPTER 3:
FORGIVENESS AND HEALING

Healing and forgiveness is a choice. There is power and freedom in forgiveness and healing. It will release you from trauma, unspoken pain, resentment, fear, and anger. If you make a choice to do the work of finding positive outlets (a therapist, a support group, a mentor, etc.), you will be able to reap the benefits of internal peace.

You may be wondering, "Why should I forgive when the other person hasn't acknowledged the pain they caused me?" While that is a very great question, this is not about excusing the other person's behavior. You must remember that forgiveness isn't about the other person, it's about you. If your power was stolen through this process, it's time to take your power back.

Some of us can relate to being hurt, taken advantage of, and treated like God's know what! We become immune to this and continue putting others before ourselves and giving 100% to find out that we weren't the priority in the relationship. We were abandoned and left empty without warning or notice. Our morals, values, and integrity were compromised in the process. It's even likely that you betrayed yourself and the people you loved to accommodate the relationship. Now, here you are picking up the pieces of yourself and trying to come to terms with why you were treated as such. It's time to let it go. This was part of the process. It's time to forgive yourself, and them, so you can move forward and walk into the divine light that is meant for you.

Let's be very clear: you don't need to have a relationship with the person you are forgiving. Your reconciliation is all about what you need. Once you learn the power in forgiving, it will allow you to move forward without jeopardizing your peace, altering your mental health, or impacting your freedom.

There are consequences to turning away from healing. If you let situations control you, it may cause you to unintentionally pass that trauma down to your children. **Healing is not only for you.** It is also about the generation that comes after, and the example you are setting for them. When your children grow up and act in an unacceptable manner, and you wonder why they're behaving this way, assume a bigger perspective. At some moment in time, you may have let people use and abuse you, and kids mimic what they see growing up.

True forgiveness indicates that you are healing, and that you vow to honor yourself, and no longer give power to what once held you in bondage.

Forgiveness doesn't seek revenge. **It gives you freedom!** While this is easier said than done; If you are not in a place of forgiveness, there is a huge possibility that hurt, anger, and disappointment still linger and reside within you. What this means is that self-work is required to start the process of forgiveness. The sweetest revenge is reaching your full potential and getting what you were meant to have while been at peace. Forgive and thank them for the experience.

Once you're able to forgive, it's time to start the healing process. It's not enough to just talk about your pain, trauma, or violations

FORGIVENESS AND HEALING

from your childhood or past; you must also confront it. Healing is a process, and it takes time for you to get to where you want to be. You have to be honest in the process, and understand that the road won't be easy, but it will definitely be worth it. You will no longer operate from your pain.

As you navigate your healing process, know that each person's path will look different. The first step is to be open to heal and have the awareness to acknowledge past experiences to bring you full circle to a positive future. In your time of healing, you will start to see yourself and others as flawed humans who make mistakes. You will understand your triggers and learn how to use appropriate coping skills. You will gain control and have full of awareness of people around you, and things that may have denied you peace. The pain that once held you back from loving yourself wholeheartedly will be dissolved. Pain that once resided in you will be replaced with love, faith, and peace. No more going into relationships with open wounds or with bandages. Allow yourself to heal inside and out.

What are some of your open wounds?

On the following page is an opportunity to reflect on how you need to heal and forgive. I would invite you to address your personal triggers and identify outlets to help you move forward.

INVISIBLE FREEDOM

In this exercise, please complete the activity about the chapter *Forgiveness and Healing*.

Personal Triggers: What are some behaviors, and/or situations that trigger you and affect you mentally? (*anxiety, depression, etc.*)

Personal Triggers	**Healing**	**Outlet**
Ex: *I shut down when I need to speak up for myself due to issues from my childhood.*	Ex: *Learn to take baby steps in speaking up for myself to build my confidence.*	Ex: *Seeking professional counsel, exercise, get good sleep, etc.*

FORGIVENESS AND HEALING

"The hardest walk is walking alone, but it's also the walk that makes you the strongest."

—Unknown Author

CHAPTER 4:
ME, MYSELF, AND I

Being in solitude will bring forth the undeniable strength residing inside of you. **Strength that has been hidden in the shadows for quite some time.** This journey requires you to walk alone. Yes, alone! While having a support system is necessary and great, there is power in self-healing. While walking alone can be uncomfortable, it will ultimately force you to become a better version of yourself and will support your mental health. You will be able to find your voice and become clear about how you want to operate moving forward. You will be forced to think about how to rebuild and repair from the damages you have encountered.

You will be forced to rely on God to get you through this process. Often times, we fixate on a specific person to help us overcome our circumstances. We even get upset when mom, dad, sister, brother, best friend—those who are within our reach—seem so very distant. It's because you need to be focused on the lesson that God wants you to learn. God will take us through things so that we come out stronger than before.

Ultimately, what doesn't break us makes us stronger!

Walking alone will shed light on the fact that you may be *co-dependent*. Often times trauma, pain, and insecurity cause co-dependency. When we're co-dependent, we feel like we can't ever be alone. We think we need other people to define us, or to take care of our emotional needs.

If you experience co-dependency, it may be hard for you to walk alone and be by yourself. However, it is very important. I would recommend detoxing from dating, texting, sex and reaching out to someone on whom you are dependent. The mere thought of being alone may cause you to resort to what's familiar, and in most cases, can cause you to rely on addictions. If you have an addiction of any form, it may indicate that you have pushed your pain so far back in your brain that you have to rely on something external to survive day to day. This could include using alcohol and marijuana to help you cope with the pain you're enduring.

Walking alone will clear your mind. It will help you gain a better understanding of yourself and force you to appreciate having someone in your space vs. having someone fill a void of loneliness. It also will help you stop making excuses for people who don't respect you, or themselves. You will begin to appreciate the people in your circle that help you become a better version of yourself as you develop and navigate through life.

We constantly absorb the opinions of others. And more times than not, we let the opinions of others dictate how we operate. You must learn to empower yourself through this process. You need to learn the importance of finding your voice and ultimately do what is best for you and your well-being. Keep in mind that this is a process that is learned over time.

By walking alone, you will find balance, have clarity, and unlearn bad habits that don't serve a greater purpose in your life.

Take this moment to be grateful and aware of the transformation that will happen as a result of being still for once. I encourage you to set time aside weekly to reflect deeply and personally about yourself. Perhaps this time will uncover how you can become a better person, spouse, partner, grow in your motherhood, and/or provide other insight that are important to you.

This powerful transformation only happens when you can be present within your thoughts.

INVISIBLE FREEDOM

In this exercise, please complete the activity about the chapter *Me, Myself, and I*.

A *S.W.O.T* Analysis is a brainstorming tool to identify your internal Strengths and Weaknesses and external Opportunities and Threats. This is a common practice used in business to evaluate the business and improve processes. However, it can be a great personal tool as well.

Strengths	Weaknesses
What do you expect to discover about yourself while spending time alone?	What do you think may surface while walking alone?

Opportunities	Threats
What positive expectations do you have about walking alone?	What frightens you about walking alone?

*"You usually have to wait for
that which is worth waiting for."*

—Craig Bruce

CHAPTER 5:
PREPARATION

There is something quite special about the preparation period. This is a golden opportunity to become focused on you to plan, work, and execute a positive routine of daily habits.

Often times, when we're moving fast through life, we get distracted and don't notice what we need to become the best version of ourselves. This is the perfect time for you to put yourself first and discover new things. Use this waiting period to live your best life. Invest in yourself by going to the gym, building your credit, starting a new business, paying your debt, saving for that house, spending quality time with your children, friends, and family, traveling, volunteering with organizations in your community, or going back to school. The things you haven't done or have yet to accomplish—this is your time to make them happen.

Even if you are currently in a relationship and you decide to work on yourself, it's so vital that you dedicate time for yourself and the people you love and care for. That way you create balance and to keep the momentum going while creating a healthy balance throughout all your intimate relationships.

As you elevate to a higher version of yourself, this unique transition period is going to force you to watch the company you keep. Some people won't understand that you are in a transition, and that you are vowing to become a better version of yourself. During this preparation period, make sure you have positive people around you, and remain optimistic about who you can become.

Just because you are in the process of healing and reflecting does not mean that you are desperate. It's your choice to wait. Often times we wait around on a man to tell us when he is ready. After he is done having his fun and eliminating his options, he wants to insert himself in your life with no genuine intentions, unchanged behavior, and without being healed himself. He's ready to interrupt your life and force his agenda and dump his childhood traumas on you. Sometimes he may even go as far as to judge you for being emotionally mature.

Remember: you're not waiting for someone to pick you. You are the pick! And don't you forget that.

Don't have the mindset of emptiness or limitation. Take this time to build yourself up. If you don't, it will make it hard for you to decipher wolves in sheep's clothing.

Don't be misled.

Focus.

Focus.

Focus.

On the following page, reflect on ways to support yourself while you wait.

PREPARATION

In this exercise for the chapter *Preparation* write a list of things that you would like to accomplish during this time. Or, write down things you need to give more time to.

1. _____

2. _____

3. _____

4. _____

5. _____

6. _____

7. _____

8. _____

9. _____

10. _____

"You have to learn to say no without feeling guilty. Setting boundaries is healthy. You need to learn to respect and take care of yourself."

—Unknown Author

CHAPTER 6:
THE POWER OF NO

Have you ever found yourself saying "Yes" to any and everything because you felt that you couldn't say NO?

If you answered "YES," you are not alone. The power of saying no will help you learn to be honest and consider your feelings while also maintaining healthy boundaries within your relationship. In the long run you're doing yourself a disservice by saying yes when you really want to say no. While it may cause you to feel uncomfortable, saying no can be very empowering. Sometimes in relationships you feel as if you must conform to your partner's every need. However, it is okay to not always agree or feel obligated to do something when you simply don't want to.

If your partner asks you to do something, it's perfectly normal to simply say, "Not today, I'm tired." Or you're busy, or you'll get back to them, or honey, do you mind doing it today?

We need to be mindful of what we agree to in the moment. You don't want to say yes to something and set yourself up for a lifetime of regret. An example of this could be not setting boundaries in the beginning of a relationship and your partner being inconsiderate and complacent.

Saying the word "no" may awaken your anxiety and cause you to feel uncomfortable, because you may feel like you're disappointing your partner. But if you learn the power of no, it can save you years of regret, resentment, and time.

This is a moment for you to be honest with yourself and your partner so that it will ultimately benefit the both of you. If you are not careful, your partner can become co-dependent, and instead of a partner, it will feel like you're raising a defiant child. The goal is to be loving, supportive, available, open, and caring within the relationship, while at the same time not losing sight of prioritizing yourself.

We unconsciously create a comfortable environment for others and spoil them without realizing that our "yes" is not being reciprocated. Be sure to *balance* your yes's and no's. If you don't, you may feel unappreciated, undervalued, or unloved. If you only focus on pleasing your partner, you will end up displeasing yourself in the process. When you agree to something, make sure you can maintain it for the years to come.

If you struggle to say no, there's a possibility that you generally struggle to communicate your needs within the relationships. In this process of learning to say no, you may have to sit your partner down and converse with them. Tell them about your difficulty. It's not that you don't want to do things for them, just not all the time. And the reason you have a hard time expressing yourself isn't because of them, but something you went through in your past. Hopefully, that will give them insight into your feelings and how to support the relationship moving forward.

This may sound silly, but practice saying no in private. Stand in front of the mirror and get comfortable saying no. It will help when you have to say it to someone else.

THE POWER OF NO

Establishing personal boundaries with the power of no is an important part of any relationship—it ensures that you both have each other's best interest at heart, and that you share a mutual understanding. Saying no doesn't have to be mean, rude, loud, or aggressive. It can be done with compassion and understanding. *All it simply means is that when you answer yes, it will come from your heart.*

Trust me, you will be okay! They will be okay!

INVISIBLE FREEDOM

In this exercise, please answer the following questions about the chapter *The Power of No*.

Why is it hard for me to say No?

Why is it important for me to say No?

How do I feel when I say No?

THE POWER OF NO

What are the benefits for me by saying No?

What will I gain for saying No?

"A person that is a Master of patience is a Master of everything else."

—George Savile

CHAPTER 7:
PATIENCE IS A VIRTUE

Is patience hard for you?

In society today, we live in a world of instant gratification. We want an immediate fix for everything: personal goals, relationships, finances, career, parenting, etc. This type of instant fix fuels our ego and satisfies our emotions, but it can come at a dangerous price. It's short-lived most of the time. Think about this in terms of relationships. How many relationships have you been in because you were tired of being lonely? You wanted someone to love you right now. You wanted to feel like you mattered right now. You wanted to prove to society that someone loves you.

It's okay, there is no judgement here. Now, I have one question to ask you—are you still in that relationship? If you answered no, this is where the skillset of patience comes into play. It's important to exercise your ability to be patient.

Patience allows you to be more conscious of your decisions and have better self-control. While it may feel like a slow start, especially in relationships, you will start to appreciate the depth patience offers. With time, you will come to know the internal workings of your partner, instead of being completely focused on their exterior. This is one of the secrets to a deep relationship.

Timing is everything.

INVISIBLE FREEDOM

If you are not mentally, physically, emotionally, and spiritually ready for someone to enter your life, there is no need to rush. The person you find will not serve your purpose and long-term desire for a healthy relationship, because you will attract what you left behind in your past. Things you haven't healed will pop up like toast in a toaster. Then you wonder… how did I get here again?!

If you want real love, real friendships, and real connections in your life from this day forward, learn the importance of patience. You'll feel even more grateful when things work out in your favor on their own timeline. You started this journey with the hardest part: focusing on yourself before stepping into a relationship. Now, it's time to let all that work marinate. Continue building your foundation and stay focused on your goals. The right person will come along… don't go searching for them. Remember there are layers to people that only shed over time. You now know that you won't settle for less than what you truly deserve.

Being impatient will destroy all of the great inner work you've done and cause you to miss out on what is waiting for you. Don't be eager, thirsty, or desperate. Remember, God said in His word, "Love is patient and kind." (1 Corinthians 13:4)

PATIENCE IS A VIRTUE

In this exercise, please answer the questions about the chapter *Patience Is A Virtue*

1. How would patience help you?

2. What benefits will come from being patient?

3. What have you learned from being impatient?

4. How do you currently practice patience? (*Search- ways to practice being patience*)

*"The way I feel is that there is a balance
in my life between being alone and interacting
with people, between being and doing."*

—Eckhart Tolle

CHAPTER 8:
WELLNESS CHECK

Often times when we are going through life changes, we want to remove ourselves from the world. This can help us process our emotions and be vulnerable by ourselves, without judgement or interruptions. When we seclude ourselves, we often think that people don't understand or get us, and that they may use what we share against us in the future. We even think we are a burden to others, so we'd rather go through it all alone.

You should always believe that at least one person understands you and will support you. Even the strongest people need to be uplifted and supported.

It's totally fine to isolate, but if you are not careful, isolation can become a breeding ground for negative thinking. It can descend to destructive levels you would not be able to fathom. This can lead to depression, loneliness, and emptiness. You need to know how to stay balanced. It can be helpful to consider that there are two forms of isolation:

1st form: Positive Isolation – This is your time to recharge, become laser focused on your priorities, strengthen your ability to be empathetic, understanding, and passionate about your goals. Isolation keeps you from the distractions of the world and helps you understand yourself on a deeper level.

2nd form: Negative Isolation – This kind of isolation involves sitting with your thoughts for too long. Now, negative thinking is starting to seep into your mind. You've totally disconnected yourself from every fiber of your being. If you're not careful, it can lead to depression and anxiety.

When you need to have a moment by yourself, which form would you prefer? Hopefully you chose the first one. However, you may be asking yourself, "How do I get out of the 2nd form should I go down that road?"

That is a very great question, and one that can be solved by having an accountability partner. What if you could have a friend, family member, or loved one conduct wellness checks when they haven't heard from you? Ultimately, they can be responsible for getting you moving again, and helping you refocus on what is important to you.

On the following page is your opportunity to put your accountability plan together. Don't rush this process. Really allow yourself to think about the people you hold near and dear, and who can help you during this period.

WELLNESS CHECK

In this exercise for the chapter *Wellness Check*, I want you to write down 1 to 5 people that can hold you accountable and do wellness check-ins. If they notice that you are in isolation, and it is affecting you in a negative way, they must reach out.

Make sure you inform your accountability partner of this exercise, and give them detailed information about what to look for when checking in. You don't have to talk about why you're in isolation, but it is important that you feel safe. Be sure to inform them of ways you like to communicate, whether it's verbal, text, or visual.

Example: "It's been 5 days; I haven't heard from you. I'll be by to take you to get ice cream. (You have to commit to the wellness check.)

1. _____

2. _____

3. _____

4. _____

5. _____

"Communication to a relationship is like oxygen to life. Without it... it dies."

—Tony Gaskins

CHAPTER 9:
EFFECTIVE COMMUNICATION

Did you know that ***active listening*** is one of the key components of communication? Active listening forces you to repeat back what you've heard and allows you to hear the needs of others and demonstrate that you are aware of their emotions versus your own interpretation of what you think you heard.

The problem is most of us never learned how to communicate effectively. We simply learned how to talk to get our point across and be right. Often times we communicate in defense mode. We've yelled, become angry, been aggressive, completely shut down, or simply wanted to be right all the time. By learning to listen, and demanding that you are heard, you will be able to build trust, reduce arguments, have a mutual understanding, clarify your feelings, and deal with disagreements more respectfully.

To be an effective communicator, it's important to know your communication style. The four most common communication styles are:

Passive – *Accepting or allowing what happens or what others do, without active response or resistance.*

Aggressive – *Ready or likely to attack or confront; characterized by or resulting from aggression.*

Passive-Aggressive – *A type of behavior or personality characterized by indirect resistance to the demands of others and an avoidance of direct confrontation, as in procrastinating, pouting, or misplacing important materials.*

Assertive – *Having or showing a confident and forceful personality.*

When these different communication styles interact, there can be conflict. If you have a passive communication style, and your partner is passive-aggressive, you approach situations differently.

No matter your style, when navigating conflict, an effective communication tool is "I" statements. "I" statements concentrate on the feelings, beliefs, and actions of the person speaking, rather than making it about the person receiving the message. It helps especially with people that tend to be defensive.

An example of an "I" statement is: "I feel unappreciated and frustrated when you leave your clothes lying around for me to pick up." Instead of simply blaming the other person for their actions, you approach the conversation by stating how this behavior makes you feel or impacts you. It diverts attention from blaming and turns towards a shared desire to address the situation.

As you navigate your communication style, it's important that you avoid non-verbal communication. Non-verbal communicators usually talk with their body language and shut down when they have to use words. It isn't until deep problems fester and rise to the surface that you may say things out of anger to hurt your partner.

Being an effective communicator will help you get through challenging times within any relationship. It will also build your confidence. Your partner should not have to read your mind to know how you feel in order to fulfill your needs, and vice versa.

EFFECTIVE COMMUNICATION

If you fail to communicate properly, someone will want you to see things their way. For some of us, another person has controlled the narrative, and it may feel as if you don't know how to think or speak for yourself. It's not because you didn't have anything to say, but because you choose not to argue and be confrontational. The other person might get upset when you respond in a way that's not to their liking. When you finally start speaking up for yourself, they may not value or respect your truth.

It's important to deal with conversations and disagreements, and to learn to communicate effectively. Prevent your partner and others from thinking they have some form of control over you. Practice boundaries, and communicate them.

Developing a healthy communication style is multi-faceted. You will learn how to respectfully speak to someone, how to demand to be addressed with respect, and how to verbalize your concerns in a healthy manner. It's important for you to listen, process what you're hearing, put your ego aside, speak up for yourself, and remember that one person doesn't get to control the narrative of the conversation.

Following this page is your opportunity to reflect on your style of communication.

INVISIBLE FREEDOM

In this exercise, please complete both activities about the chapter *Effective Communication*. Think about a situation with your partner that caused conflict or is still causing conflict. Then, fill out the sentences in a way that focuses on "I" statements.

ACTIVITY 1: I STATEMENT

Example: *I felt* hurt when you yelled at me.

When I was at my friends, I didn't like how you spoke to me.

I need you to be more patient with me.

Could you please stop being so rude to me?

(Feelings)
I Feel _____

(Situation)
When I _____

(Needs)
I need _____

(Request)
And could you _____

EFFECTIVE COMMUNICATION

ACTIVITY 2: COMMUNICATION SKILLS

In this exercise, write down ways to hold yourself accountable to becoming a better communicator and listener.

How can I develop my communication skills?

1. _____

2. _____

3. _____

4. _____

5. _____

"The biggest coward is a man who awakens a women's love with no intention of loving her."

—Bob Marley

CHAPTER 10:
WHAT'S THEIR INTENTIONS?

Intentions and behavior go hand in hand and must be demonstrated over time.

When you know someone's intentions, you become clear about what they really want and need from you. **Don't ignore it**. The question you have to ask yourself is, is that something you can offer?

Sometimes we give people the benefit of the doubt until we're proven wrong. It's not enough to make assumptions about someone's intentions. You need clarity. Knowing someone's intentions will create a sense of respect, boundaries, and you'll know that this person values you and your time.

Often times, people are molded by life experiences and when they experience a certain level of pain and/or betrayal- they tend to live in it. Sometimes it becomes difficult for them to look past the experience of the hurt they've endured. So, instead of learning and healing from what hurt them in the past, they carry that unresolved baggage in all their relationships and operate in pain. This behavior alters the intent of someone and controls how they love, value, and treat others. While they may love and want the best for you, their learned behavior won't allow them to.

INVISIBLE FREEDOM

It is impossible to have the intentions to love someone while shielding yourself from change. The reason being is that someone will get hurt in the process and loving someone requires one to be unselfish. That's why it's important to take your time to get to know someone before investing in the relationship so that you are aware of their intentions. Even in a healthy relationship you will have hurt. However, it will look different when you embrace it. It becomes growth pain.

Don't be so caught up in your feelings and emotions that you get attached to someone and they don't feel the same about you. Sometimes people are not ready to commit. Don't force it. Just as you are in preparation now, there's someone preparing for you.

In today's world, we all have our own personal agendas. It takes time to discern someone else's motives towards you. Some people have positive agendas. Some people have negative agendas. Some people have hidden agendas. It's ultimately up to you to make sure that this person's intentions best suit your needs.

The best way to understand someone's intentions in a relationship is to truly spend time with them. You will be able to understand their true character, values, and morals.

Don't ignore the signs. If someone has displayed selfish, inconsiderate, and self-centered behavior, and they only come around to get their needs meet, they probably don't have good intentions for you. You can't make someone love, like, or respect you. They can't make it up—it has to be in them. While we may talk to our partners about their intentions, they might lie or not fully know themselves. However, the truth always comes out in someone's behavior. That's where we can look for honest information.

WHAT'S THEIR INTENTIONS?

The more time you spend with someone, the more their true self starts to surface. You're probably thinking that people usually show you what they want to show you, and perhaps what you fall in love with may not be the entire picture. To some degree this is true, but more times than not, different flags go off when you meet someone.

You know exactly what they are.

The red flag means you need to run away now. The yellow flag means something is not sitting right with your spirit, and you must proceed with caution. The green flag means both of your auras are connected and have a mutual understanding and respect for each other.

I want you to drill this word into your head: Discernment. Discernment. Discernment. This is going to be your best friend. As you begin to travel down this road of finding that special person, don't betray yourself to gain someone's love and attention.

They have to work for it.

You probably know someone who has been in this scenario, or maybe you have: at the start of the relationship, you briefly talk with your partner about being exclusive, but then decide to be friends with benefits. This is where the danger comes into play. During that time, feelings begin to grow, and subconsciously you can fall into a role of "spousal/girlfriend duties" without ever being a spouse, let alone a girlfriend. Our natural nurturing habits as women can be taken for granted. Don't let people use and take advantage of you. There is someone designed just for you.

Do you know someone like this? The person who has invested all her hope that this will blossom into something long-term, but ultimately is being neglected in the process. The man has become accustomed to the natural nurturing routine without wanting to commit to being exclusive.

Does this sound like a situation you want to be in? If you answered, no… give yourself a round of applause.

To avoid falling into this situation, you must clarify and understand this person's intentions for you. You have to learn to look past their exterior and ask those meaningful questions early on. These are questions only you can decide based on what you're seeking and how you want to be supported through the relationship. For some, these questions can fall into the areas of mental health, dreams and aspirations, and morals and principles.

The worst thing you can do is not ask and end up being misled and hurt. It's equally important that you learn to move according to the person's actions. That will be the indicator for you to set the tone of your relationship. We typically ignore the everyday actions of a person over the persona we've created in our minds to satisfy our comfort.

Pay attention to the behavior.

WHAT'S THEIR INTENTIONS?

In this exercise, please answer the questions about the chapter *What's Their Intentions?*

What questions do I need to ask my partner about commitment?
Ex: Do you want an exclusive relationship?

What questions do I need to ask my partner about their intentions?
Ex: We have been dating for a while, what are your intentions for me?

What questions do I need to ask my partner about relationship expectations?

Ex: What are you looking for in a partner? Ex: What is a deal breaker for you?

"Love, friendship, laughter... some of the best things in life, really are free."

—Bob Marley

CHAPTER 11:
FRIENDS BEFORE LOVERS

Meeting someone and establishing a friendship is important. It will allow you to get to know this person on a deeper level.

Often times, we're attracted to someone's physical appearance, personality, or materials things, such as their financial status. But when you get the opportunity to become friends with someone first, you're able to connect with their soul. You can see what they stand for (integrity), and how they respond and conduct themselves to different life situations.

In the process of developing this friendship, time is a big factor. It's crucial that you take your time while building this relationship, and to not rush it to simply have the title. There is a unique advantage if you play your cards this way because you get to be in control. It will give you the ability to make the decision to eliminate who and what you don't want in your life. It also allows you to look beyond the surface of the individual because you're simply building a friendship.

When you start as friends, expectations are low, and there is no pressure to be someone that you're not. If you start from a dating lens, you may unconsciously portray an image of yourself that is not your everyday personality. Hear me closely: there is nothing wrong with starting off as friends. Building friendships should be embraced.

It's equally important to note that even in the process of dating, you continue to make time for the things and people you enjoy and love. You must remember the people who were there for you when you weren't pursuing this new-found relationship. How many people do you know who are guilty of giving their all to a new relationship, only to forget about their inner circle? Don't become that person. Find balance.

In the previous chapter, I mentioned the importance of Discernment *(The ability to judge well)*. Again, this word is going to become your best friend. Here's the thing… create what you can maintain throughout the relationship. You never know if you may end up being together, or if this person will become your life partner and spouse. People can easily adapt to patterns, behaviors, and routines. Should a shift arise while you are dating, it can trigger trust issues and bring up insecurities. You want to be able to know what these are as you build rapport.

On the following page, you will have an opportunity to reflect on the positive and negative characteristics you notice when building a friendship.

FRIENDS BEFORE LOVERS

In this exercise for the chapter *Friends Before Lovers*, write down positive and negative characteristics that you notice about the friendship.

Positive characteristics	Negative characteristics

*"She fell in love with his soul before
she could touch his skin.
If that isn't love, then what is."*

—Bianca Lamarre

CHAPTER 12:
REAL LOVE

The time has come for you to apply what you have learned from your journey of self-discovery to find your soul mate. Finding love is a beautiful thing, especially when you have learned to love yourself first.

You've been able to learn that we should not be taken advantage of and that we should know someone's intentions before investing too much of ourselves. In this chapter, we are going to identity the difference between love and lust, and how to release your fears. This will allow you to let your guard down and welcome this person in.

You will learn how to distinguish love from lust. Lust doesn't serve a purpose in your life, and you will no longer operate from your emotions to satisfy your insecurities. You have come too far to please your flesh. You are no longer looking at the exterior of someone; you can feel in your soul if they are the one. You have witnessed their consistency in loving you over time.

On this journey of discovering and receiving love, it may feel unfamiliar, but you deserve it! Don't let your past behavior interfere with your opportunity to experience real love. You have been working on yourself, and you learned how to give and obtain love. Now that someone cares, trusts, accepts, supports, nurtures, and respects you… be sure to embrace it. If you find yourself rebuilding brick walls due to trust issues, refer to Chapter 3, *Healing and Forgiveness*, to help you heal and use tools when you're triggered.

I encourage you to remember one thing through this journey:

Love is an action word.

It requires work. It requires consistency. Remember that you learn and grow from all experiences in your life. You should ultimately be what you desire in a relationship. It's not enough to survive in a relationship with just love—it needs to be nurtured, demonstrated, and displayed.

Love is patient, love is kind, it does not envy, it does not boast, it is not proud. It is not rude, it is not self-seeking, it is not easily angered, it keeps no record of wrongs. Love does not delight in evil but rejoices with truth. (I Corinthians 13:1)

While things may sometimes be complicated, know that you will have times in your relationship when you will be pushed to become a better version of yourself. You will be uncomfortable at times, but it's a part of your journey. Just when you believe you have all the answers, *boom*, another level of growth is required to get you to the next level in your life. Embrace it! Love will support your growth.

When you exude love, when you walk in love, you will attract love.

You deserve love. It awaits you.

REAL LOVE

In this exercise for the chapter *Real Love*, you will write ways to identify love and lust, and how to remember the differences.

Love: An intense feeling of deep affection or to be deeply committed and connected to someone or something.

Lust: A very strong sexual desire.

When someone loves you, how should they show up?	*What does lust feel like and how does it show up?*

INVISIBLE FREEDOM

*"In one lifetime, you will love many times,
but one will awaken your soul forever."*

—Unknown Author

CHAPTER 13:
LOVE IS IN THE AIR

Whoever has your heart has your attention.

The time has finally come. You have found someone with whom you want to spend the rest of your life with. Everything you've been through has aligned you for this very moment. The both of you feel connected, your souls are aligned, your vibe is unmatched, and both of your hearts are connected.

You have been through it all. You doubted God. You loved God. You lost. You won. You cried. You smiled. You've been sad. You've had joy. You've been positive. You've been negative. You've been heartbroken. You've picked up the pieces. You wanted to give up, and yet you got up and had faith even when you wanted to quit. All in all, you fought for your sanity.

These experiences make the journey even more rewarding. We are not exempt from going through this rollercoaster called life. This is a never-ending process. I want to share some words of wisdom with you from my grandmother: *"It's not what you go through, it's how you go through it."*

As you continue to love…

Remember you're flawed.
Remember you're healed.

INVISIBLE FREEDOM

Remember you're imperfect.
Remember you're blessed.
Remember you will forever be growing.

You will have to become familiar with each other in your relationship. You will have to learn new things about each other, and be open to different way of growth. You will have to find ways to meet your own needs and theirs.

Understand that everyday won't be perfect, but with love, understanding, communication, and the will and desire to actively work for each other's love, you will be just fine. With God, all mountains can be moved and barriers can be broken.

Love doesn't require you to be perfect. **Love** requires you to have compassion. **Love** requires you to love yourself. **Love** requires you to have empathy. All so that you can love others. Be sure to nurture yourself as well as your partner.

Celebrate each other.
Pray with each other.
Laugh with each other.
Support each other's dreams.
Support each other's goals.
Support each other's growth.
Don't give up on each other.
Grow with each other.
Maintain your individuality, always!

LOVE IS IN THE AIR

In this exercise for the chapter *Love is in the Air*, get a mason jar and write positive affirmations, bible scriptures about love, and all things inspiring on a piece of paper. Place them inside the jar. When you feel doubt creep in, pull a note out and remember how far you have come, then pray and/or meditate.

"Just like the lotus we too have the ability to rise from the mud, bloom out of the darkness and radiate into the world."

—Unknown Author

CHAPTER 14: *SOAR*

You should be proud of yourself, you made it through! Now that you are dating, open to dating, or ready for a new start in your current relationship… DON'T LOSE YOURSELF! Keep God first, create balance, and remember to keep stability within your current social and personal life.

It's important to have a support system and people that will create a safe space for you, and keep it REAL. This support system should be honest, transparent, supportive, non-judgmental, loving, and caring. Your newfound love will be happy to love you, cherish every moment, and enjoy this new journey. There will be times that the old you may show up, and that's okay. Use the tools and resources you've learned over time. **You are human.**

You will have challenges, disagreements, and misunderstandings in your relationship, but now you have the tools and the resources to make healthier choices. With God's everlasting Love, Grace, and Mercy He will see you through. Be sure to pray, meditate, take care of your mental health, and refer back to the exercises you completed in this book. Remember the strength that resides inside you. Make healthy choices, create good habits, and count your blessings.

INVISIBLE FREEDOM

Throughout this process, you learned new things about yourself. You now have information that will carry you through many relationships—intimate, personal, and even business relationships. You are now knowledgeable in this area of your life, and know how to show people how to treat you. You have made the choice to experience only healthy relationships. You know who to call on when you are going through peaks and valleys in your life.

Let's be clear: pain is inevitable. Without pain, you have no experience; and without experience, you don't evolve.

God is within her; she will not fall.

(Psalms 46:5)

SOAR

In this last exercise for the chapter *Soar*, create a vision board and get a journal. On your vision board, add positive affirmations, pictures, and other things that you want to manifest in your life.

To achieve it you must see it, speak it, write it, and believe it.

Vision board materials may include, but are not limited to:

Board
Glue Stick
Magazines
Mementos/Pictures
Pens/Pencil
Scissors
Stickers

You are a woman of strength, courage, and dignity.

One who values herself and fights for what she believes in. A woman who will not give up on her dreams regardless of how many obstacles stand in the way.

If that does not make you beautiful, then I don't know what does.

—Facebook @ Joyofmom